Sisters

A Book of Quotations

To have a loving relationship with a sister
is not simply to have a buddy or confidante;
it is to have a soul mate for life.

Victoria Secunda

For there is no friend like a sister
In calm or stormy weather;
To cheer one on the tedious way,
To fetch one if one goes astray,
To lift one if one totters down,
To strengthen whilst one stands.

Christina Rosetti

The desire to be and have a sister is a primitive and profound one that may have everything or nothing to do with the family a woman is born to. It is a desire to know and be known by someone who shares blood, history, dreams, common ground and the unknown adventures of the future, darkest secrets and the glassiest beads of truth.

Elizabeth Fishel

Other things may change us,
but we start and end with the family.
Anthony Brandt

Parting is all we know of heaven
And all we need of hell.

Emily Dickinson

The only causes of regret are laziness, outbursts of temper, hurting others, prejudice, jealousy and envy.

Germaine Greer

Don't be afraid of the space between your dreams and reality. If you can dream it, you can make it so.

Belva Davis

Among the merits and the happiness of Elinor and Marianne let it not be ranked as the least considerable, that though sisters, and living almost within sight of each other, they could live without disagreement between themselves or producing coolness between their husbands.

from Sense and Sensibility by Jane Austen

Lo, the lilies of the field,
How their leaves instruction yield!
Hark to Nature's lesson given
By the blessed birds of heaven!
Every bush and tufted tree
Warbles sweet philosophy —
Mortal, flee from doubt and sorrow;
God provideth for the morrow.

Heber

W ithout a family, man, alone in the world,
trembles with the cold.

André Maurois

Sisterly love is, of all sentiments, the most abstract.
Nature does not grant it any functions.

Ugo Betti

True kindness presupposes the faculty of imagining
as one's own the sufferings and joys of others.

André Gide

Appreciation is a wonderful thing;
it makes what is excellent in others belong to us as well.

Voltaire

I am only one; but still I am one.
I cannot do everything, but still I can do something;
I will not refuse to do something I can do.

Helen Keller

We tell the ladies that good wives make
good husbands; I believe it is a more certain position
that good brothers make good sisters.

Samuel Johnson

The who do not know how to weep with
their whole heart don't know how to laugh either.

Golda Meir

Dream as if you'll live forever.
Live as if you'll die tomorrow.
James Dean

When you get into a tight place and everything goes against you till it seems you could not hold on a minute longer, never give up, for that is just the place and time that the tide will turn.

Harriet Beecher Stowe

Far away there in the sunshine are my highest
aspirations. I may not reach them, but I can look up
and see their beauty, believe in them,
and try to follow where they lead.

Louisa May Alcott

Reproof a parent's province is;
A sister's discipline is this:
By studied kindness to effect
A little brother's young respect.

Mary Lamb

We have no more right to put our discordant states of mind into the lives of those around us and rob them of their sunshine and brightness then we have to enter their houses and steal their silverware.

Julia Seton

One is taught by experience to put a premium
on those few people who can appreciate you
for what you are.

Gail Godwin

The ineffable joy of forgiving and being forgiven
forms an ecstasy that might well arouse
the envy of the gods.
Elbert Hubbard

There is nothing like staying at home for real comfort.

Jane Austen

When I was at home, I was in a better place.

Shakespeare: As You Like It

. . . the affectionate heart which could not bear
to see a sister slighted on the smallest point.
from Sense and Sensibility by Jane Austen

A good natured man has the whole world
to be happy out of.

Alexander Pope

Maybe we are less than our dreams,
but that less would make us more than some Gods
would dream of.

Sister Corita Kent

The happiest conversation is that of which nothing
is distinctly remembered, but a general effect
of pleasing impression.

Samuel Johnson

What a lot we lost when we stopped writing letters.
You can't reread a phone call.

Liz Carpenter

You can accomplish by kindness
what you cannot do by force.
Publilius Syrus

Ah, but a man's reach should exceed his grasp –
or what's a heaven for?

Robert Browning

You grow up the day you have your first real laugh,
at yourself.

Ethel Barrymore

Beauty comes in all sizes, not just size 5.

Roseanne

A ministering angel shall my sister be.

William Shakespeare: Hamlet

I go walking, and the hills loom above me,
range upon range, one against the other. I cannot tell
where one begins and another leaves off. But when
I talk with God, He lifts me up where I can see clearly
where everything has a distinct contour.

Madam Chaiang Kai-shek

'To walk three miles, or four miles, or five miles,
or whatever it is, above her ankles in dirt, and alone,
quite alone! whatever could she mean by it? . . .'
'It shews an affection for her sister that is very pleasing.'
from Pride and Prejudice by Jane Austen

A word, once sent abroad, flies irrevocably.

Horace

Great anger is more destructive than the sword.

Indian (Tamil) Proverb

What do we live for, if it is not to make life
less difficult for each other?

George Eliot

Anger as soon as fed is dead,
'Tis starving makes it fat.
Emily Dickinson

Though I know he loves me,
Tonight my heart is sad;
His kiss was not so wonderful
As all the dreams I had.

Sara Teasdale

The next day is the first link of the chain
which fetters a man in a gang with thousands
to that superfluous anxiety which is the evil one . . .
This anxiety the bird has not.

Soren Kierkegaard

There is no home that is not twice as beautiful
as the most beautiful city.
West African Proverb

The family – that dear octopus form whose tentacles
we never quite escape.

Dodie Smith

The more we know, the better we forgive.
Whoe'er feels deeply, feels for all that live.

Mme de Stael

The young ladies entered the drawing room
in the full fervour of sisterly animosity.

R S Surtees, Mr Sponge's Sporting Tour

You are never given a dream without also
being given the power to make it true.
You may have to work for it, however.

Richard Bach

Are there any brothers who do not criticise a bit
and make fun of the fiancé who is stealing
a sister from them?

Colette

Each has his past shut in him like the leaves
of a book known to him by his heart, and his friends
can only read the title.

Virginia Woolf

I always felt that the great high privilege,
relief and comfort of friendship was that one
had to explain nothing.

Katherine Mansfield

What is beautiful is good,
and who is good will soon be beautiful.

Sappho

One who knows how to show and to accept kindness
will be a friend better than any possession.

Sophocles

The only way to get the best of an argument
is to avoid it.
Dale Carnegie

A beautiful face is of all spectacles
the most beautiful.
Jean de la Bruyère

'Had I died, in what peculiar misery should I have left you,
my nurse, my friend, my sister!—You, who had seen
all the fretful selfishness of my latter days; who had known
all the murmurings of my heart!—How should I have lived
in your remembrance? . . . I shall now live solely for my family.
You, my mother, and Margaret, must henceforth
be all the world to me.'

from Sense and Sensibility by Jane Austen

We are not only sisters. It is an amazing and sort of doubly strong association to be linked instinctively (and by environment, early life, etc.) and by one's desire and reason. It is a rare relationship. I feel as though you have leaned down and lifted me up to where you were so many times. At least if we have had many things together your having them first or at the same time has helped me to realise and comprehend better what was happening.

Anne Morrow Lindbergh in a letter to her sister, 1928

There is only one happiness in life,
to love and be loved.

George Sand

Sisters never quite forgive each other
for what happened when they were five.

Pam Brown

'We must stem the tide of malice, and pour into
the wounded bosoms of each other, the balm
of sisterly consolation.'
from Pride and Prejudice by Jane Austen

Blood's thicker than water,
And when one's in trouble
Best to seek out a relative's open arms.

Euripides

Y ou find yourself refreshed by the presence
of cheerful people. Why not make an honest effort
to confer that pleasure on others?
Half the battle is gained if you never allow yourself
to say anything gloomy.

Lydia M Child

Once you can laugh at your own weaknesses,
you can move forward. Comedy breaks down walls.
It opens up people. If you're good, you can fill up
those openings with something positive. Maybe you
can combat some of the ugliness in the world.

Goldie Hawn

The Lord watch between me and thee
when we are absent from one another.

Genesis 31:49

By compassion we make others' misery our own,
and so, by relieving them, we relieve ourselves also.

Sir Thomas Browne

The best and most beautiful things in the world
cannot be seen or even touched.
They must be felt with the heart.

Helen Keller

W hen our relatives are at home, we have to think
of all their good points or it would be impossible
to endure them.

George Bernard Shaw

Endow the Living – with the Tears –
You squander on the Dead.
Emily Dickinson

With a sister, one can never fear that success
will go to one's head.
Charlotte Gray

Life isn't a matter of milestones but of moments.
Rose Fitzgerald Kennedy

We pardon as long as we love.

François de la Rochefoucauld

That is the happiest conversation where
there is no competition, no vanity, but a calm,
quiet interchange of sentiments.

Samuel Johnson

To know after absence the familiar street and road
and village and house is to know again
the satisfaction of home.

Hal Borland

There's no vocabulary
For love within a family.
Love that's lived in
But not looked at,
Love within the light of which
All else is seen,
The love within which
All other love finds speech
This love is silent

T S Eliot

For all the blessings life has brought,
For all its sorrowing hours have taught,
For all we mourn, for all we keep,
The hands we clasp, the loved that sleep,
We thank Thee, Father: let Thy grace
Our loving circle still embrace,
Thy mercy shed its heavenly store,
Thy peace be with us evermore

Oliver Wendell Holmes

Better to bend than to break.

Scottish Proverb

If you judge people, you have no time to love them.

Mother Teresa

Keep your eyes on the stars,
and your feet on the ground.
Theodore Roosevelt

Lord, grant that I may always desire more
than I accomplish.

Michelangelo

That best portion of a good man's life,
His little, nameless, unremembered acts
Of kindness and of love.

William Wordsworth

The real art of conversation is not only to say
the right thing in the right place but to leave unsaid
the wrong thing at the tempting moment.

Dorothy Nevill

Love is the emblem of eternity; it confounds
all notions of time; effaces all memory of beginning,
all fear of an end.
Madame de Stael

When you reach for the stars, you may not quite
get one, but you won't come up with a handful
of mud either.

Leo Burnett

One of the most adventurous things left us
is to go to bed. For no one can lay a hand on our dreams.

E V Lucas

How wonderful it is that nobody need wait a single moment before starting to improve the world.

Anne Frank

An ounce of blood is worth more than a pound
of friendship.
Spanish Proverb

The only thing a heated argument ever produced
is coolness.

American Proverb

The future belongs to those who believe
in the beauty of their dreams.
Eleanor Roosevelt

W orse than idle is compassion
If it ends in tears and sighs.
William Wordsworth

Sisters stand between one
and life's cruel circumstances.
Nancy Mitford

The outside world doesn't have a lot to offer.
You have to make your own heaven in your own home.

Bette Midler

Do not be anxious about tomorrow;
tomorrow will look after itself.
Matthew 6.34

Sometimes when one person is missing,
the whole world seems depopulated.

Lamartine

'Lord, how often am I to forgive my brother
if he goes on wronging me? As often as seven times?'
Jesus replied, 'I do not say seven times;
I say seventy times seven'.
Matthew 18:21-22

Family quarrels are bitter things. They don't go
according to any rules. They're not like aches
or wounds, they're more like splits in the skin
that won't heal because there's not enough material.

F Scott Fitzgerald

As a woman I have no country.
As a woman my country is the whole world.
Virginia Woolf

Our deeds determine us,
as much as we determine our deeds.
George Eliot

Always be a little kinder than necessary.

James M Barrie

A sister is both your mirror – and your opposite.

Elizabeth Fishel

Throw your dreams into space like a kite,
and you do not know what it will bring back,
a new life, a new friend, a new love, a new country.

Anaïs Nin

Family faces are magic mirrors.
Looking at people who belong to us, we see the past,
present and future.

Gail Lumet Buckley

The words the happy say
Are paltry melody
But those the silent feel
Are beautiful.
Emily Dickinson

Where you go, I will go, and where you stay,
I will stay. Your people shall be my people,
and your God my God. Where you die, I will die,
and there I will be buried.

Ruth 1:16-17

Laughter is the closest distance between two people.

Victor Borge

Loyalty brings its own reward.

Proverbs 11:17

Life is either a daring adventure or nothing.
To keep our faces toward change and behave like free
spirits in the presence of fate is strength undefeatable.

Helen Keller

Forgiveness is the answer to the child's dream
of a miracle by which what is broken is made whole
again, what is soiled is again made clean.

Dag Hammarskjold

W hen people say: she's got everything,
I've only one answer: I haven't had tomorrow.
Elizabeth Taylor

W hat value has compassion that does not take
its object in its arms?

Saint-Exupéry

Generosity gives assistance rather than advice.

Luc de Vauvenargues

The quarrels of friends are the opportunities of foes.

Aesop's Fables

The greatest thing in family life is to take a hint
when a hint is intended – and not to take a hint
when a hint isn't intended.

Robert Frost

If you're going to be able to look back
on something and laugh about it, you might as well
laugh about it now.

Marie Osmond

You don't choose your family.
They are God's gift to you, as you are to them.
Desmond Tutu

P ractice random acts of kindness
and senseless acts of beauty.
Adair Lara

A home is no home unless it contains food and the fire
for the mind as well as for the body. For human beings are not
so constituted that they can live without expansion.
If they do not get in one way, they must in another, or perish.

Margaret Fuller

Love has nothing to do with what you are expecting to get —
only what you are expecting to give — which is everything.
What you will receive in return varies. But it really has
no connection with what you give. You give because you love
and cannot help giving.

Katherine Hepburn

To jealousy, nothing is more frightful than laughter.

Françoise Sagan

Our hours in love have wings; in absence crutches.

Colley Cibber

Comparison is a death knell to sibling harmony.

Elizabeth Fishel

Family is the most effective form of government.

Robert Half

And all the loveliest things there be
Come simply, so it seems to me.
Edna St. Vincent Millay

Follow your instincts.
That's where true wisdom manifests itself.
Oprah Winfrey

The fragrance always stays in the hand
that gives the rose.

Hada Bejar

If I have to, I can do anything.
I am strong, I am invincible, I am Woman.
Helen Reddy

When we were children, we used to think that when
we were grown-up we would no longer be vulnerable.
But to grow up is to accept vulnerability . . .
To be alive is to be vulnerable.

Madeleine L'Engle

To look up and not down,
To look forward and not back,
To look out and not in, and
To lend a hand.

E E Hale

Kindness effects more than severity.

Aesop's Fables

Most quarrels amplify a misunderstanding.

André Gide

In every woman there is a Queen.
Speak to the Queen and the Queen will answer.
Norwegian Proverb

I tried always to do better: saw always a little further.
I tried to stretch myself.

· *Audrey Hepburn*

Nature made us individuals, as she did the flowers and the pebbles; but we are afraid to be peculiar, and so our society resembles a bag of marbles, or a string of mould candles.
Why should we all dress after the same fashion?
The frost never paints my windows twice alike.

Lydia Maria Child

'It's such a comfort to know that someone loves me
so much, and feels as if I'd helped her.'

'More than anyone in the world, Beth. I used to think
I couldn't let you go; but I'm learning to feel that
I don't lose you: that you'll be more to me than ever,
and death can't part us, though it seems to.'

from Good Wives by Louisa May Alcott

We cannot really love anybody
with whom we never laugh.

Agnes Repplier

To live is so startling it leaves little time
for anything else.
Emily Dickinson

They sicken of the calm, who know the storm.

Dorothy Parker

Where there is great love there are always miracles.

Willa Cather

No one can make you feel inferior without your consent.

Eleanor Roosevelt

You are as welcome as the flowers in May.

Charles Macklin

In every part and corner of our life,
to lose oneself is to be the gainer; to forget oneself
is to be happy.
Robert Louis Stevenson

No stranger can get a great many notes of torture out
of a human soul; it takes one that knows it well –
parent, child, brother, sister, intimate.

Oliver Wendell Holmes, Sr.

'If Cassandra were going to have her head cut off,
Jane would insist on sharing her fate.'
her mother, of Jane Austen